About two thousand years ago some astronomers saw a new star in the sky. 'I think it means that a great new king has been born,' said one.

They decided to follow the star. So they prepared for their long journey. Camels and horses carried food and gifts for the new king.

For days and weeks the star led the way. The travellers crossed deserts and mountains. They rode through rivers, fields and forests.

At last they reached the great city of Jerusalem. Messengers from the palace of King Herod rode to meet them.

The wise men told King Herod about the star. 'It will lead us to the greatest king there has ever been,' they said.

King Herod was angry. He invited the important men of Jerusalem to his palace. 'What's this I hear about a baby who is going to be the greatest king in all the world?' he shouted.

King Herod asked the wise men to let him know where to find the child. 'I would like to visit him,' he lied. They agreed and set off again.

The star appeared in front of them. Then, suddenly, it stopped above a house in Bethlehem. They had reached the end of their journey.

They knocked at the door, and a man came to open it. 'We've travelled for weeks, following a star, to see a special baby,' they told him.

The man led them inside. They saw the little child, Jesus, who was there with his mother. Then they laid down their gifts and left.

That night the wise men all had the same dream. An angel appeared to them, warning them not to go back to King Herod.

Joseph, too, had a dream. 'King Herod wants to kill little Jesus,' an angel told him. 'Take the baby and his mother to Egypt where you will be safe.'

When King Herod found out that the visitors from the east had tricked them, he was furious.

But the wise men were far away, joyfully praising God on their journey home to the east.

Jesus, Mary and Joseph had already escaped; they were safe.

Palm Tree Colouring Books are drawn by
Arthur Baker

The other titles in the series are

The Welcoming Party
Noah's Big Boat
Jonah and the Big Fish
The Lost Son
Jesus goes to a Wedding
God makes the World
Daniel and the Lions
The Good Samaritan
The Lost Sheep

© 1996 Kevin Mayhew Ltd

ISBN 0 86209 875 0
Catalogue No. 1300010

KEVIN MAYHEW LTD
Rattlesden
Bury St Edmunds
Suffolk IP30 0SZ